footprints in the sky

geof pearson

tigersun books

First published in Great Britain in 1992

by Tigersun Books
    PO Box 382
    Kingston upon Thames
    KT2 5YN

Cover illustration by Simon Scarsbrook

British Library Cataloguing-in-Publication Data.
A catalogue record for this book
is available from the British Library.

c C

Photoset by Jaggerprint, Kingston upon Thames
Printed by Cox & Wyman, Reading

600 373 0308

ISBN 0 9520297 0 7

DATE DUE FOR RETURN

28. 06 95

This book may be recalled
before the above date

90014

contents

robinson crusoe

the whole town
had heard that
robinson crusoe
was attempting
to sail around the world
in a little boat
he had made himself
and the whole town
gathered to wish
robinson crusoe
well

robinson crusoe
had not intended
to sail alone

he had placed
an advertisement
in the local paper
'wanted:
young blonde
with large bosom
to accompany
handsome traveller
around the world'

robinson crusoe
received plenty of replies
but the ladies were put off
when he showed them his little

boat
he had built in the
middle of a public garden

no one could understand
how he would get his boat
down to the docks
let alone sail it
around the world

but the girls
underestimated
robinson crusoe's ingenuity

he had cut a hole
in the bottom of his boat
and poking his legs through
he walked his boat
out of the gardens
through the town
and down to the docks
to great cheering
from the crowd

robinson crusoe
still had critics
and none more
than mr johnson

'you are a fool
robinson crusoe
that boat will founder
on the high seas'

but crusoe had supporters too
'robinson crusoe
does not know
the meaning
of a word like founder'

so mr johnson
ran home for his dictionary
but by the time
he returned
robinson crusoe
had set sail
on his epic journey

blue buses

mr johnson
(a distant relative of
   the man who invented the dictionary)
was waiting at the bus stop
at the first stage
of his journey around europe

he was so excited
he kept looking at his
ticket

'I hope the buses
are running on time today'
he said

but it was not to be
mr johnson   waited

and   waited

and   waited

and   waited

the air was cold
his face blue
and the wind strong

so strong
it blew the bus stop over
which hit mr johnson
fatally on the head

it was a temporary bus stop
(but a permanent death)

then a blue bus came along
'room for one more only'
said the driver

mr robinson stepped over
mr johnson's body
and took his place
on the bus
for the trip around europe

the egg

beneath a photochemical smog
an egg grew and grew
before it began to crack

a large naked man
very well endowed
emerged

'they should arrest him
for gross indecency'
said mrs gibson
(putting on her glasses
to get a better look)

the naked man
sprinted down the motorway
faster than any car

'do you want a job'
said a pizza house manager
'you can deliver our
express pizzas anytime'

'we will give you
lots of money'
said the glucose company
'if you say
you drink our product'

naked ladies
lining his route
slowed him down
for a little time
(while he admired the scenery)
then he accelerated again

'lets all bask in his glory'
cried the nation
'the olympic games are coming'
'let him run for england'

'let him run for england'
'let him run for england'
echoed the nation
waving union jacks

but when the naked man
reached dover
he sprung off
the white cliffs
and leapfrogged
for france

pissarro

poor pissarro

the beautiful girl
who posed for him
loved him
bore him seven baby
pissarros
had turned into a
    bad tempered
    difficult
    aggressive
    wife

only painting counted
to pissarro
but his wife thought
he should get a proper job
to feed the family

'you ought to get a proper job
to feed the family'
she would shout at him
'nobody likes your painting
- look at that young girl
  who won one of your paintings
  as a prize in the raffle:
  she soon swapped it
  for a cream bun'

'what's for dinner?'
asked pissarro

'nothing - not a scrap
that's what being married
to an artist means'
said his wife

'I'd love a juicy steak'
said pissarro

'we haven't a sous
and you would like a steak?'

'a juicy steak
with red wine
please'
said pissarro

poor pissarro
didn't get his steak
but he did do
a marvellous sketch
of his wife
in a violent rage
attacking him
with her fists
and shouting
'piss off pissarro!
piss off pissarro!'

red lips

after millions of years
without a rest
the sun took a day off
(only one day, mind)

in her place
a gigantic pair of red lips
posed all day

word soon travelled the
world of this momentous event

in england
excited people
set their alarm clocks
found their cameras
       telescopes
       artists palettes
some climbed mountains
to get a better view
but they were disappointed
(it was cloudy all day)

in spain
everybody had a marvellous view

'we do not allow clouds in spain, señor'
'bulls are placed all along
the pyrenees to blow them away'

the view at dusk
was wonderful
red lips setting on a spanish sea

but when the lips
kissed the sea
they started drinking
(it must be thirsty work
deputising for the sun)

soon the mediterranean
that took a hundred thousand years to fill
disappeared

by midnight
you could walk
from spain
to africa

where the sea had once been
only a few piscine-shaped pools remained

each pool
reflected
the sky full of stars
full of the light
of years and years

not one absentee
among them
till tomorrow

rodin's lovers
(the kiss)

one day
rodin fell asleep
with a lump of clay
in his hands
and dreamed of
ancient greece

when he awoke
the lump of clay
had transformed
into a marvellous sculpture
rodin's lovers

every second of
every day of
every year
rodin's lovers
embraced
but the earth
never moved for them

then one day
the tectonic plates
that controlled their passion
collided
and rodin's lovers
finally felt the
earth quake
beneath them

unfortunately
rodin's lovers
did not escape
the experience
undamaged

only a small
piece fell
from the male
but sadly the
earth will never
move for them again

rodin's dream
(the birth of the seahorse)

poseidon
god of the sea
surveyed burning troy
shimmering in the aegean

the city
poseidon himself built
stone by stone
was in ruins

nothing remained
which didn't bleed
and poseidon
was very angry

steam
erupted
from his
ears
nostrils
mouth and
other parts
(too rude to mention)
until he evaporated
into a huge angry spirit
clouding the sky

poseidon
wanted to avenge troy
zeus
cautioned against it

zeus said the trojans
were equally to blame
as the greeks
for the war

'the greeks are
tired of war
and want only
to return home and
embrace their wives'

poseidon
was not convinced
so they arranged
to test the greeks

'when the greeks
row home
pegasus will fly
low over them
if they harm
an innocent horse
I, zeus
will unleash my
most powerful thunderbolt
to add to your storms
but if they rejoice
at seeing pegasus
then we will both
grant the greeks
a safe passage home'

so pegasus flew
over the greek boats
her wings
casting beautiful rainbows
on the sea below

but the habits
of war die hard
and the greeks
hurled spears
one nicking
pegasus
in the leg

while
poseidon and zeus
unleashed a merciless storm
upon the greeks
pegasus
flew as far as she could
away from the aegean
until she rested
near the confluence
of two great rivers

there pegasus
spent the summer
recuperating from her wound

but when a rainbow
appeared
pegasus decided she
must return to the land
where she was born
to give birth herself

sadly pegasus
was struck by lightning
and was never seen again
though the waters
where she perished
were full of seahorses
the like of which
had never been seen before

the sheep

a stray sheep
called shomulus
was walking
down the high street
when he went
into the butchers

the butcher's face
lit up
but the sheep knew
not all smiling faces
are friendly
when the butcher
chased after him
with a cleaver

the sheep escaped
hiding by the river
but unfortunately
fell in

most sheep drown
when they fall in
but shomulus flourished

he fed
on seaweed
and seahorses
and he grew
and grew and grew
until he was much bigger
than any ship that sailed
down river

the sheep was
very kind to ships
and helped them
in fogs

only occasionally
would he be
a little naughty
and munch
an odd sailor
or two
to liven up his diet

one day
shomulus
grew tired
of sitting on the river
and headed for the
open sea

shomulus
was never seen again
some say he headed
towards finland
most say he was
captured off
the flemish coast

it is true
some little thin belgians
became big fat belgians
in some otherwise
inexplicable metamorphosis

dermot and antlanticus

atlanticus
was so tall
that flat on her back
her wavy hair
lapped manhattan harbour
while her feet
could be tickled
from the west coast of ireland

she was in this
transoceanic repose
when dermot set out
with the aim
of making love to her
somewhere in the
middle of the ocean

in the longest period
of foreplay
in the history of mankind
he tickled every
hair on her leg
and was rewarded
with her responses
which gave birth
to a new generation
of behaviour

dolphins made poetry
which rhymed with
the rhythm of the waves
salmon sang
the most beautiful melodies
imaginable to man
porpoises
with each swish of their fins
began to cleanse the styed seas

unfortunately for dermot
it was not he
who excited atlanticus
but an erotic octopus
who had wrapped
his tentacles around her thighs
and excited atlanticus so much
with clitoral delight
that she raised her knees so high
that dermot slid
all the way down her leg
and was last seen
crawling out of the sea
near galway bay

wigan on thames

mr robinson had a
marvellous scheme
so that southerners
could experience
northern life
without travelling too far

cotton mills
clogs
cloth caps
gas lamps
knocker-uppers
wigan pier
uncle joe's mint ball factory
should be moved
cobble by cobble
two hundred miles south
by the thames

a marvellous scheme!
or so he dreamed!
a trip that's not too dear!
from waterloo
day return
by train to wigan pier!

south of glasgow

'I wouldn't eat a
railway sandwich
if it was ......'

it wasn't very tactful
for mr mcbain
to say
he would never eat a
railway sandwich
just as the
catering assistant
was wheeling
her trolley
along the train

mr mcbain
remembered
the last time
he had a bacon sandwich
on the train

it was in the days
when the driver
cooked eggs and bacon
on the firebox
of his steam locomotive
and then passed the sandwich
along the train
from passenger
to passenger

until it reached
its destination

'the last sandwich
had more grit in it
than bacon'
grumbled
mr mcbain

poor mr mcbain
the euston to glasgow train
was very late
very very late
delayed by snow
in the scottish mountains

in the end
mr mcbain
was so famished
he was forced
to eat his words
(and a railway sandwich)

the illusionist

a huge crowd
lined the scottish streets
to witness
the great illusionist's
funeral

some believed he had not
really been trapped backstage
when the empire theatre
caught fire
and that this was to be
his greatest illusion

the funeral procession was late
but worth waiting for

four horses
their colours constantly changing
preceded a coach
with an open glass coffin

a little boy sitting on his
father's shoulders
looked into the glass coffin
and said
'why are they going to bury him dad
when he's been cremated already?'

out of the coffin
flew doves
that filled the sky
and turned
to handkerchiefs
that fell
like rain
to dry
the tears
of the crowd
below

when the great illusionist
reached his burial place
a score of widows
each called mabel
each believing herself to be
the one and only illusionist's wife
bore testimony to
his illusionary powers

then the chief mourner
a dog
(also called mabel)
cried the obsequies while

the great illusionist

levitated

above his
glass coffin

and the world began to spin faster
and faster and faster and faster
and a thousand years flew by
in a few seconds

and the clothes peeled from the mourners
and the flesh peeled from the mourners
and the air became dense and smoky
and the skeletons became black
and then the illusionist finally
laid to rest

when it was over
the skeleton of mr gibson
said
'that was a jolly good funeral
one of the best I've attended'
mr robinson had to agree
'one of the best' he said

viking sandwich

the viking and mr robinson
were enjoying dinner
mr robinson made polite conversation
'the pork has
a lovely flavour'

the viking explained
that the pork tasted of apples
because the pig had been fed on apples
'you are what you eat' he said

the viking's wife
was vegetarian and
she was eating strawberries
mr robinson
looked wonderingly
at her

the viking
was very keen
to prove his
'you are what you eat' theory

'if you make love to my wife
her fragrance will be that
of strawberries'

'I can't believe it'
said mr robinson

so the viking invited
his wife and mr robinson
to remove their clothes

soon they were making love
and though a smell of
strawberries wafted through
his nostrils
mr robinson denied the smell
so as to prolong the lovemaking

'I must join you'
said the viking
'to see for myself'

mr robinson looked a little worried
until he realised
that the viking's wife
was the filling in the sandwich
and the three
made love together

at length
mr robinson could not deny
when he closed his eyes
he could have been
in a bed of strawberries

'that proves it'
said the viking
'that proves it
you are what you eat!'

his wife
kept silent
she was much too polite
to mention
the scent of her lovers

before clouds

before clouds
were born
trees rained
all over sweden

swedes liked trees
and
trees liked swedes

trees provided
drinking water and
protection for man
from the biting winds

man provided trees
with protection
from the roaming elk
that stripped their bark

when clouds
were born
swedes hated clouds
that stopped
the sun from shining

and clouds
hated the bond
between swedes and trees

that is why
in thunderstorms
clouds tell the lightning
to strike trees
especially those
with swedes
sheltering
beneath

midnight sun

dave had been warned
not to lay on the beach
in the midnight sun
but he knew best

'the sun may shine
for twenty four hours a day
but the sun is weak
in finland
and won't burn me'

so against advice
dave lay in the midnight sun
and fell asleep

in the morning
dave was still there
on the beach
beneath a swarm of
blood-sucking mosquitoes
his skeleton
wrapped in white skin

and he was quite right
the midnight sun
didn't burn him

the streets of prague

milan
dreamed of marrying a girl
who one day
would self combust

milan
imagined holding hands
walking
the streets of prague
when suddenly
she explodes
BANG!
and he is left staring at
smoking shoes

instead
he married maria
who didn't self combust
but did have a fiery temper

one day
milan told maria
that he considered
self combustion
such a good idea
it was a wonder
god didn't think of it himself

'think of how much
would be saved on coffins'

milan
hated coffin makers
and those who made
rich pickings from death

milan told maria
that he would have
loved to marry
a girl who would self-combust

this was a great mistake

'so I'm second best am I?'
exploded maria
and she slung
her stilletto heeled shoes
at milan
(and killed him)

after a few hours
maria had chopped milan up
and was burning him
piece by piece
on an open fire

as milan's
burning skull
flickered in the fireplace
casting
shadows on the wall
she remembered
how milan hated coffins

'I'm sure' she said to herself
'he'd applaud what I'm doing
if only he could
see me now
(and I hadn't
chopped his hands off
and burned them)'

poem for stalin

'glasnost is bunkum'
said the russian poet
to his wife
'what was wrong
with the good old days
of joseph stalin?'

it was ironic
the poet said that
he had once written
a poem for stalin
stalin liked poetry normally
but he didn't like this poem much

it was probably the bits about
his big mouth and
big teeth and big nose
and big ears and
squinny yellow eyes
he didn't like much

'it was a good job
you signed the poem
boris pasternak'
said the poets wife

poor old boris
it was a good job
stalin had a big brain
to match his big nose and ears

he knew boris
wouldn't dare write
such a poem
and sign it

poor old boris
he still wasn't spared
off he went to the labour camp
to help the secret police
compile a list
of all the poets
in the land

a million poets
were on the list
and a million poets
were marched to the forests
in perfect metre and
    perfect rhythm and
    shot

'it was a good job'
said the poet's wife
'it was a good job
that neither boris pasternak
nor the secret police
nor anybody in russia
considered you a poet'

blue train
(without underpants)

olga had a husband
(vladimir)
who kept
a secret diary

it was a good job
it was secret
because stalin would
not have been pleased
if he knew
what vladimir
had written about him

olga also had a lover
(dmitry)
who brought
excitement

dmitry made love like a steam locomotive
'and what do steam locomotives have olga?'
dmitry would ask
'a tender behind'
olga replied

then olga pulled down dmitry's underpants
and spanked his bottom
till he had
a tender behind

as they made love
dmitry made
train noises
'chuff, chuff, chuff, chuff
chuff, chuff, chuff, chuff
chuff, chuff' mixed
with wild whistles
and the sounds of
trains passing through tunnels
across bridges and past
a wonderful pussy
in the fields

olga loved these
love making journeys so much
she wanted them more often
so she wrote a secret note
to the secret police
about vladimir's
secret diary
hoping vladimir
would be sent to siberia
for a year or two

the secret police
came in the middle of the night
saw what vladimir
had written about stalin
took him to a nearby forest
and (unfortunately for vladimir)
his life was over
in a shot

olga was heartbroken
she had not meant
vladimir's life to end like that
and although dmitry
still made love to her
she didn't want him
to be a steam locomotive
any more

she wanted him to make love
like vladimir used to

and she wanted dmitry
to keep a secret diary
like vladimir used to

dmitry agreed
but it was quite sad really
he only ever wrote
about two things

first   - how he wished
          he could be a
          steam locomotive again

second - what a very nice man
          joseph stalin was

hungary for love

'and who gave you authority
to call yourself
a lover?' the judge demanded

'no one' ferenc replied

the judge
was a woman
it was a new age
women were in power
in hungary
and no man
could make love
without a certificate
without risk of imprisonment

'women have suffered too long
from the inadequate
selfish
fumblings of man
on love's sweet instrument
men
whether they love study
or not
must study love'
the judge preached

'but I am an exception'
ferenc pleaded
'a natural lover
heir of appollo'

'what do you know of
feletio
jismification or
love with a capital T?'
the judge demanded

'I know of all those things'
he said
(though he took care to
point out that
he had never practised
love with a capital T)

'and I know of
yonirise and
zoogonimy' said ferenc

the judge
was a fair woman
and had never heard
of zoogonimy
(though she pretended
she had)

'there is only
one way to settle this case'
the judge said
'take off your clothes!'

in the middle
of the courtroom
ferenc demonstrated
the art of zoogonimy
and in no time
the judge
sweetly moaned
from her discovery
of love's new song

ferenc had proven
he was a natural lover
and had no need
of a certificate
but the judge
still had him locked up
like a beast
in a cage
without food or water

'I'll let him
out myself later'
she said to the jailer
'I want to be
zoogonised again'
she thought to herself

blue flash

cricket isn't played between
england and romania now

matches between the two countries
were always full of arguments

the romanians didn't like
english umpires who said
they were caught by the wicketkeeper
when the ball had not even
touched the bat

the romanians
were only prepared to play england
if an electrical device
was fixed to the bat
which gave
a small blue flash
if the ball
caught the edge of the bat

they knew a count
in transylvania
who knew a lot about bats
and he knew somebody
who was very good
with electricity
(he'd even brought
a cannibalized man to life)

the english agreed
and the romanians
were very pleased

without hindrance
from english umpires
diaconescu and ionescu
made nearly 600 runs
on the first day of play

then diaconescu got an
almighty edge
which carried the ball
to white
fielding at third man
and produced
not a small blue flash but
a big blue flash

there was no doubt
diaconescu was out
as the record
in wisden testifies:

diaconescu   (electrocuted)
c white   (electrocuted)
b wilson   (electrocuted)
322

poles apart

poland
is the land
of sexual equality

a woman miner
is treated
the same as
men

at the end of
a hard day's toil
she showers
like the men

her clothes
are kept dry
and free of
coal dust
like the mens
in the roof
of the changing room

and when she is ready
her clothes are hoist down
by a man who turns a wheel

it is true
the man who turns the wheel
finds her
naked beauty
attractive
and
lowers
her
thrilly
panties
more
slowly
than if they belonged to
jozef or leopold or lech

on the surface
poland is the land of equality
but deep down
the laws of nature
cannot be usurped
unlike poles attract

white sunday
(5th march 1916)

mr robinson
was retelling
otto
a war story
his grandfather
had told him

a zeppelin
was making
it's dirigible way
through a snowy night
when it dropped
....

'oh, let's not
talk of when
we were enemies
now we are friends'
interrupted otto

'let's pretend
you had paper guns
not to shoot the zeppelin down
but to blow sweet nothings
heart-shaped sweet nothings'

'and let's pretend
the zeppelin
had come
not to drop bombs
but to deliver
red roses for
the arms of
your beautiful ladies

red roses for
the chimney pots of
your charming houses

red roses
for your
white fields
below'

'oh - it's still
snowing is it?'
asked mr robinson

'let's not change
history too much
for the sake
of friendship'
the german replied

the president's ball

'students at this university
know' said the president
'that we have a long tradition
of eating a professor
at our ball'

this year
you have chosen
the professor of german
professor hargreaves
for swearing
too much
in lectures

hargreaves
wasn't pleased
and shouted
'you shits
you shits
you sodding
        shits'
as he was
whizzed off
to the kitchens

before anybody
could eat their
main course
starring professor hargreaves
the president's bodyguard
(a huge black cat)
had to verify
the meat on offer was
the professor of german

by tradition
the huge black cat
ate the brain

the cat
soon gobbled up
the brain

if it was
the professor
the cat
would now have
a first class honours degree
in german

there was a long silence
then the cat spoke

'sie sind scheisse
und shitzhausen und
shitzhausen und scheisse'
said the cat

the cuckoo

in a little
swiss town
a man had
a son who
loved cuckoo clocks

he loved the little cuckoo
and dreamed one day
he might be a little cuckoo

sadly the little boy died
and the clock went wrong

it took the father
twenty years to
overcome his grief
and take the clock
to the clock maker
to see if it
could be repaired

the clock maker
twiddled this
twiddled that
and breathed new life
into the clock
and in no time
the clock restarted
where it once left off

such a marvellous job
did the clock maker do
that the man went to the cemetery
and when nobody was looking
he dug up a small coffin
and carried it
to the clock maker

'this is my son' he said
'he died many years ago
can you breathe new life
into my boy
like you did to the clock'

the clock maker
twiddled this
twiddled that
and breathed new life
into the boy
and in no time
life restarted
where it once left off

his father was overjoyed
but the clock maker
spoke a cautionary word

'your boy will be fine
he will run and jump
and play and have fun
but from time to time
he might be a little cuckoo'

53

custody of the moon

'good morning
mr schizophrenic!
I take my hat
off to you
(but not to you)'
said the psychiatrist

the psychiatrist
hadn't been too balanced himself
ever since his wife left him
but the schizophrenic
was still surprised
to see the psychiatrist
on his own couch

'you can be the psychiatrist
and I'll be the patient'

the psychiatrist
had a shrunken planet
which orbited his room

how he had shrunken it
was a mystery

once the psychiatrist
also had a shrunken moon
whose lunar light
shone so beautifully
on his desk and spectacles
- but his wife took it

'she took custody
of my son and
    my moon
when she left me
and all I can think of now'
said the psychiatrist
'is my wife
making love
in the viennese moonlight
to some handsome
stag beetle'

'oh - did I forget to tell you'
said the psychiatrist
'I shrunk my wife too
- that's why she left me
- that's why she wants a divorce
- that's why she finds
    stag beetles so attractive'

the night watch

night after night
rembrandt worked hard
painting his picture
of the night watch

but when it was finished
those fine men
who guarded amsterdam
didn't like their portrayal
in rembrandt's picture

only the captain
and his lieutenant
van ruytenburch
liked the picture
(they were in the
 centre of the action
 commanding the guardsmen)

the guardsmen
didn't like the picture

'it's too dark'
complained one guardsman
'and it's too big'
complained another

even though
the darkest bits were cut
from the edges of the picture
which made it
lighter and smaller
the guardsmen
still didn't like it

indeed
many years later
when a mad knifeman
attacked the night watch
not one guardsman moved

if van ruytenburch
hadn't come to the rescue
the night watch
might have been
cut to ribbons

the cheeselovers

holland
is a marvellous country
for cheeselovers

where else
can you still smell
faint wafts of
nineteenth century edam
and
at the same time see
van gogh's worn out boots
still steaming
in tulip fields?

where else
each lunar month
does a man
climb a giant tulip
and change
the old moon
for a moon with a
brand new flavour?

where else
is there a country
so safe for cheeselovers
that you can take
your cheese sandwich
out for lunch
knowing only one of you
will survive
and never fear
that it might be
the cheese sandwich?

the mirror principle

as a token
of their friendship
the italian people
presented the dutch
with a painting
by their most famous
living artist

the picture
was unveiled at a great ceremony

'thank you
for this truly wonderful
piece of modern art'
said the dutch president
'it will be kept
in a place of honour
in our parliament building'

it was not long though
before one or two people
said they didn't
really like the picture

'who is it anyway?'
they asked
'it seems to change
depending on how
you look at it'

not long later
everybody was saying
the picture was ugly
and should be removed

'we can't give the
italian people their
picture back
- it would be most
ungracious'
said the president

'can't we say
there was a fire in parliament
and unfortunately
the picture was destroyed'

'and that was the
only thing destroyed?' asked the president

the president
thought of a better idea
and invited
the italian artist
to the netherlands

the artist
thought he was to be presented
with an award
and while
the dutch saturated him
with wine
he tried to compose
his 'thank-you' speech

after the drink
had overflowed
the dutch president
explained the position
without telling the artist
everybody thought his picture
was ugly

then he handed
the picture
back to the artist

the italian was sad

a little boy
saw the picture
when the italian
was walking
head down
to his hotel

'look at that
picture mummy
isn't it ugly
isn't it downright
ugly'

the embarrassed mother
knew something
about modern art
and tried to make up
to the artist

'what is the
title of your picture?' she asked

'it's nothing' said the artist
'just a self portrait'
he added
even more sadly

hanno

raphael painted masterpieces
so when the pope
wanted his pet elephant painting
he naturally turned to .....
raphael

the pope
imagined how much better
his elephant
would look in patches of
reds
yellows
purples and
greens
instead of dowdy grey

raphael knew
the elephant
would use a lot of paint
and he didn't want
to use all his colours
but there was one
colour he had a lot of
- so he used that

when the pope saw
what raphael had done
to his pet elephant
he was not pleased

'a white elephant!
 a white elephant!
 what's the sodding use of
 a white elephant!'
 he raged

never again
did raphael
receive any work
from the pope
and had to return
to painting
masterpieces

napoleon

venetian pigeons
were eating
in st mark's square

suddenly
a cloud of birds
burst upon the scene

whistling *the marseillaise*
they were
much bigger pigeons
and soon pecked
the native venetian pigeons
to death

the biggest
of the french pigeons
was napoleon
(he was five foot long)

a venetian man
wasn't going to
let these
foreign birds
get away with it
so he decided
he would fight
napoleon

unfortunately
napoleon
was too strong
and held down
the venetian man
while pecking
at his flesh

napoleon
ate
his   arms
        legs
        thighs
        liver
        kidney
        brains
        heart
and eyes

in fact
napoleon
bonesapart
ate everything

dosserville

mr robinson
passed by
dossers in the street
and didn't throw a coin
in their direction

if he tossed
a small coin
it would go towards booze
and if he dropped
a gold coin
the dosser
might get up
off his smelly arse
and kiss him

mr robinson
dreamed of contributing
to a grand scheme
building a town especially
for dossers
dosserville
where instead of statues
of famous citizens on street corners
where instead of sculpture
in town squares and public parks
there would be
giant tureens of potatoes
giant cans of ale

giant bins of bread
giant bowls of soup
giant cups of tea
for dossers to help themselves

mr robinson would even build
a giant washing machine
and help throw the dossers in
(and watch them
spin round and round
with some piranha fish
for an hour or two)

the land of legs

as mr robinson
stepped off the blue bus
onto the streets of rome
a man came up to him
and said
'I know where you come from
.... the land of........'

mr robinson interrupted
'the land of green ginger'

'no! no!' said the roman
'the land of green ginger
is fine
if you like looking at
solicitors
bankers
accountants
but I prefer ladies' legs!
- and where better to see them
  than the land of legs'

mr robinson
looked mystified

'you've been all around europe
on your blue bus
and you don't even know
your home town'

the land of legs
is a nightclub
where after a few drinks
you have the perfect excuse
for lying flat on your back
in the middle of the dance floor
where if you keep your eyes open
you will see
why it's called
the land of legs
as lanky ladies
step over you
for a few moments
(till the bouncers
chuck you out)